Recreation

JULIAN ROWE

RIGBY
INTERACTIVE
LIBRARY

Interiors designed by **AMR**
Illustrations by Art Construction
Printed in the United Kingdom

00 99 98 97 96
10 9 8 7 6 5 4 3 2 1

Library of Congress Cataloging-in-Publication Data
Rowe, Julian.
    Recreation / Julian Rowe.
        p. cm. – (Science encounters)
Includes bibliographical references and index.
Summary: Discusses some of the scientific principles and technological advances
involved in such recreational activities as visiting an amusement park, backpacking,
watching television, and water sports.
        ISBN 1-57572-092-2
        1. Science—Juvenile literature. 2. Sports—Juvenile literature.
[1. Science. 2. Recreation. 3. Sports.] I. Title. II. Series.
Q163.R65 1997
688.7—dc20   96-33352
                                                             CIP
                                                             AC

Acknowledgments
The publisher would like to thank the following for permission to reproduce photographs.
Tony Stone Images, p. 4, p. 5, p. 9, p. 10, p. 14, p. 15, p. 24; Science Photo Library, p. 8, p. 12;
Zefa, p. 12, p. 23, p. 26, p. 28; Topham Picturepoint, p. 13; Image Bank: p. 17; Frank Spooner
Pictures, p. 18; Sipa Press, p. 19; Allsport, p. 20; Hulton Deutsch, p. 23; Peter Bentley/PPL,
p.25; Action-Plus, p.27

Every effort has been made to contact copyright holders of any material reproduced in this book.
Any omissions will be rectified in subsequent printings if notice is given to the publisher.

CONTENTS

THE SCIENCE OF FUN

Did you ever think that having fun had anything to do with science? If not, then think again. Recreation is all about enjoying free time, but many of our pastimes would not be possible without the help of science. The benefits of science are everywhere. We take it for granted that we can be entertained in our homes at the flick of a switch. Even outdoor activities such as hiking and sailing use science to help make better and safer equipment. But recreational activities have not always been so high-tech. What did our ancestors do for entertainment?

In the Past

Our earliest ancestors probably had very little time for fun. They spent most of their lives in search of food and shelter. But we know that in about 3000 BC, the Ancient Egyptians began to use music and dance as part of religious rituals, to ask for the gods' protection against evil or for success in hunting. In this way, music and dance gradually became part of daily life, and much later people began to enjoy these activities just for fun.

At about the same time, Ancient Egyptian priests also began to act out the tales of the gods. However, it was the Ancient Greeks who actually invented the theater. These great open-air theaters had rows of stone seats arranged in tiers like a modern sports stadium. This seating arrangement gave everyone in the audience (up to 15,000 people) a good view. Prizes were awarded for the best plays, much like the modern Oscar awards.

ACOUSTICS

Greek theaters were skillfully designed and constructed to have good **acoustics**. This meant that sound from the stage could be heard clearly by all the people in the audience, no matter where they sat. Even the smallest sounds could be heard all the way at the back!

Entertainment and Sports

The world of recreation has not changed overnight. Over the years, new developments in science and technology have been applied to traditional sports and recreational activities, to help participants play harder, go faster, and push themselves further than ever before. New materials such as carbon fiber, titanium, and Gortex have been invented to make lighter and stronger equipment for outdoor activities. As a result, dangerous sports such as white-water rafting and paragliding are safer than ever before. Science and technology have also opened a whole new world of entertainment, including television, video cameras, computer games, and techno-toys. This book looks at how the world of leisure has changed with the help of new advances in science and technology.

Surfboards are designed and sculpted with great care. It takes skill and years of practice to become this good at surfing!

Equipment you can trust is essential in climbing, no matter how skillful a climber you might be.

FUN AT THE FAIR

What scientific principles are at work at the fairground? Perhaps you enjoy a ride on the bumper cars. Or you may prefer the stomach-churning roller coaster. In the Middle Ages, fairs were places where merchants sold their goods, and traveling entertainers put on sideshows. Today's fairgrounds offer a host of exciting computer games and breathtaking rides, as well as traditional sideshows, swings, and merry-go-rounds. How do these games and rides work? How do we know that they are safe? Science gives us the answers.

The first Ferris Wheel was built at Midway, Chicago, in 1893. It was 249 feet across and had 36 cars, each seating 60 people. It was named after its inventor, George Ferris.

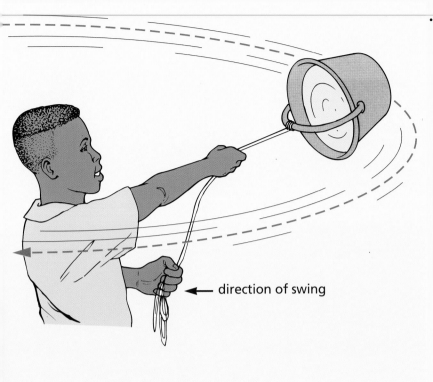

← direction of swing

Did you know that you could whirl a bucket of water on a string around in a circle without spilling a drop? As you swing you can feel a pull, or force, on the end of the string. This is called **centripetal force.** If you swing the bucket fast enough, this force is stronger than the force of gravity and keeps the water in the bucket. This same force keeps you safely in your seat on roller coasters.

Gravity is the force of attraction between earth and all objects on earth's surface. It pulls everything in toward the center of the planet. Without gravity everything on earth, including you, would be weightless and float off into space!

Gravity exists between all objects in the universe. But it is greatest for very heavy and large objects such as the sun. The sun's gravity pulls on all the planets in the solar system and keeps them moving around, or orbiting, the sun. Gravity also keeps the moon orbiting the earth.

More Circles

Some fairground rides allow you to experience "artificial gravity." You step inside a round, steel cage and stand with your back to the wall. The cage rotates, then it moves faster and faster. The floor gradually moves down, so you have nothing left to stand on. Why don't you fall? Because the rotating cage creates a force, like gravity, that keeps you firmly held against the wall.

ESCAPE FROM GRAVITY

In 1968, Frank Borman, James Lovell, and William Anders set out to travel to the moon and back in the spacecraft *Apollo 10*. They were the first people to escape from the earth's gravity.

THEME PARKS

If you want to say "hello" to a live cartoon character, visit a Viking village, meet a dinosaur, or ride on a water slide, where would you go? A theme park, of course! Theme parks are a world apart, dedicated to providing fun and entertainment. But they are also wonderful examples of how real scientific principles, and the very latest developments in technology, can be made to work for the world of recreation.

When you enter the Magic Kingdom at Disney World, anything seems possible. Thrilling rides and exciting adventures with Disney characters are made possible through the latest scientific developments.

The geodesic golf ball, "Spaceship Earth," at Disney World in Florida, is made of a steel framework covered with nearly 1,000 triangular **aluminum** panels. It stands 180 feet high and is supported on three pairs of concrete legs. It was built using geodesic principles to make the structure very strong. Inside, visitors are taken on a spiral ride through a display of important events in human history.

SPACESHIP EARTH

The geodesic golf ball, "Spaceship Earth," at Disney World in Florida, gets its name from the science of geodesy, which is all about curved lines. A curved line is the shortest distance between two points on a curved surface. Geodesy is used to study and map the surface of the world. It provides information that can be used in building, engineering, and navigation.

Virtual Reality Rides

A Star Tours adventure at Disneyland takes you on a fantastic journey into outer space without your ever leaving the park. The ride makes you feel as if you are traveling through the stars in a spaceship. It does this by tricking your body into thinking it is moving. This is easier to do than you might expect. When you look out of a train window and see a train on the next track pull out, it seems as if you are moving—in the other direction. **Virtual reality** rides make use of this sensation. "Space travelers" sit in an auditorium—the spaceship—which can be moved in different directions. Here they watch a specially shot film of outer space. Each movement on the film screen is matched by the movement of the auditorium. The resulting experience is a ride that seems like actual space travel.

MOUNTAIN BIKE MANIA

There has been an explosion in the popularity of cycling in the past 10 years, particularly with the arrival of new sports such as mountain biking. Mountain biking began in the United States. Cyclists loaded their ordinary bicycles into the back of pick-up trucks, drove up mountain trails, and rode down as fast as they could. The sport soon became very popular. So companies that make bicycles began to use new technology to develop tough, lightweight bikes to suit the rough terrain.

Mountain Bike Frames

Mountain bike frames need to be light but very strong. These days they are made from strong metals such as steel, aluminum, and **titanium.** Some frames are even made out of highly specialized materials, such as **carbon fiber,** which are used to build race cars and space shuttles. The shape of a mountain bike frame makes the bike easy and comfortable to ride.

This rider is wearing a helmet, protective clothing, and shoes. Off-road bikes have wide handlebars to give the rider more control. The space between the frame and the wheels on a mountain bike is wider than on ordinary bikes, and the wheels have no mudguards to keep mud from clogging them up.

Gears for All Terrain

Mountain bikes have lots of gears—18, 21, or 24. The low gears help the rider tackle even the steepest slopes. In a low gear, the pedals turn around very easily, but the rider has to turn the pedals many times to cover a short distance. In a high gear the rider needs to make fewer pedal turns to cover the same distance, but it is harder work. High gears are used downhill, where the terrain is smoother, to help the rider pick up speed and go even faster.

Put on the Brakes!

Mountain bikers go extremely fast, so their brakes need to be powerful. Ordinary mountain bikes have brakes that work using steel **cables.** When the rider puts the brakes on, the steel cables pull on the **cantilevers.** These push the brake pads against the wheel rims and slow the bike down. Downhill racing machines need very powerful **hydraulic** brakes, similar to those used in cars. When the brakes are applied, oil is forced down a tube and pushes the brake pads onto the wheel rim. With a hydraulic system, the brakes can be applied very hard to stop the bicycle smoothly and efficiently.

PENNY-FARTHING

The Victorians also had a bicycle to cover rough terrain. The penny-farthing, invented in 1871 by James Starley, had a large front wheel that enabled the rider to cover rough ground at high speed. The diameter of the front wheel was about three to five feet, depending on how long the rider's legs were. Modern bicycles have smaller wheels and air-filled tires to give a much smoother ride.

The most advanced mountain bike has a frame constructed from aluminum tubes with large diameters. The rounded, hollow shape makes them light and rigid. Front and rear suspensions, or springs, smooth out the ride. The steering mechanisms are sealed against dirt and are oversized for strength. As the rider changes gears, they click precisely from one to the next.

BACKPACKING

At the end of the day, when you put up the tent and light the stove, all the hard work of backpacking can seem worth while— if you have the right gear, that is! Modern outdoor clothing, boots, and equipment are made from strong, lightweight materials, using the latest technology. As a result, backpacking is a recreational activity people all around the world enjoy—no matter what the weather.

Boots Made for Walking

For short, easy walks, sneakers or walking shoes are fine. But on rough terrain hikers need strong, comfortable walking boots with stiff soles to support their ankles. Stiff soles help to prevent feet and ankles from rolling from side to side and protect the soles of the feet against stony ground. Try this simple test. Bend a walking boot from heel to toe. You should be able to do this, but not too easily. Then try to twist the heel in the opposite direction from the toe. It should not move more than about one-half inch.

burdock
seeds

VELCRO

In 1949 Swiss engineer Georges de Mestral looked through his microscope at the burdock seeds that clung to his clothing. He noticed each seed had tiny hooks that caught easily on fabric. By 1957 Mestral had invented a new product called Velcro. It consists of two **nylon** strips. One is covered with thousands of small hooks, the other with even smaller loops. When pressed together these strips stick to each other. They can also be pulled apart easily and reused.

Fabrics That Breathe

When you get wet you lose heat quickly and can get very cold. This is because water draws heat away from your body about 25 times quicker than air. It is important to stay as dry as possible when you are out in the cold, wind, or rain. Plastic fabrics, made out of nylon for example, get as wet on the inside from trapped **perspiration** as on the outside from rain. Many new waterproof materials have now been developed that can keep us dry and warm.

Today's waterproof fabrics, such as Gortex, "breathe." They have millions of tiny pores (holes) in them that let perspiration pass through from the inside, but rainwater cannot pass through from the outside.

Carrying Equipment

A strong backpack with zipped pockets and waist straps is essential for any serious backpacker. After all, there is a lot to carry—a tent, sleeping bag, camping stove, compass, first-aid kit, spare clothing, maps, utensils, and food and drink. Explorers used to need a team of people to carry all the heavy gear. Now outdoor gear is made from special lightweight material and can fold up to fit in a very small space.

ENERGY LEVELS

Scientists measure energy in **calories.** You burn about 300 calories per hour of hiking. A chocolate bar has about about 240 calories.

This tent is made from waterproof **synthetic** fabric. It has sealed seams to keep water from getting in. Flexible aluminum or **fiberglass** poles support the tent in strong winds.

ON THE EDGE

Do you enjoy a challenge? How far do you push yourself? There are some people who always push themselves further, go faster, travel to places, and do things that most people consider too dangerous. Top sailboarders and white-water canoeists can be like this. There is a whole range of recreational activities that people take part in just because they are thrilling and dangerous. They want to live on the edge. In these tests of skill and courage science is particularly important.

Have you ever seen bungee jumpers dive from platforms high up in the air and plunge toward the earth, only to bounce back up again just before their heads hit the ground? It may reassure you to learn that there is in fact a science to bungee jumping. A bungee jumper is attached to the platform by an elastic rope. When the jumper leaves the platform, his or her weight stretches the rope. It will always stretch the same amount for the same jumper. A lighter person will stretch it less than a heavier person. Bungee jumpers use three vital pieces of information—the length of the rope, the height of the jump, and their weight—to calculate exactly how long the rope needs to be for a safe jump.

White-water rafters grapple with the Grand Canyon, where waves can be 16 feet high. The inflatable raft must be steered past rocks and through rapids.

BUNGEE JUMP

Bungee jumpers use Hooke's law to make their jumping calculations. This law states that a heavy object stretches a spring twice as much as an object weighing half as much, and so on. The law was discovered by English scientist and architect Robert Hooke (1635– 1703), who did a lot of research on weights and springs.

These skydivers are forming a ring as they fall freely through the air. When they open their parachutes the air resistance is increased, and they return safely to the ground.

FREE FALLING

You might think that any falling object would pick up speed as it falls, until it hits the ground. Falling objects do pick up speed as they fall, but only until they reach a speed of about 130 miles per hour (mph). Then **friction**, or air pushing against the falling object, keeps it from going any faster. This speed is called terminal velocity. Skydivers stop falling any faster when they reach terminal velocity. They open their parachutes to return safely to the ground.

COMPUTER CRAZY

Did you know that one Ancient Egyptian Pharaoh had a version of tic tac toe chiselled into the wall of his tomb so that he could play in the afterlife? People have been playing board games for at least 4,000 years. Today all these games can be played on computer, or on a television screen, by simply plugging in controls called **game consoles.** The very first successful video game was *Space Invaders,* which came out in 1978. The makers used a familiar idea from the world of games, whereby the player has to destroy enemy invaders. But this time the computer was the opponent. This, together with the **graphics** and sound effects, gave an old idea a whole new life.

Human Brain Versus Computer

Some computer games are like traditional board games, such as checkers or chess. At first, computer chess programs were easily beaten by human chess champions. Now the best chess programs sometimes beat the champion. The computer cannot "think" like a chess player, but the computer chess program is designed to figure out the results of all the possible moves it, and the human player, can make.

COMPUTER GAMES

Computer programs give instructions to a computer or game console. The instructions are carried as long chains of numbers. These chains are coded in **binary digits** or "bits"—a method of counting that uses only ones and zeroes. The longer the chain, the more instructions it carries. The most powerful computers and consoles are able to handle longer number chains faster. The latest game consoles can handle 32-bit numbers very quickly.

Board games need only simple graphics, but some games demand a powerful and fast computer to make the pictures you see appear real.

Armchair High-tech

Some games, such as those that simulate, or imitate, flying an airplane, have very detailed graphics and need powerful equipment to make the pictures appear real. The newest consoles have CD-quality sound, can generate 16 million different colors, and operate at amazingly high speed. How do they do this?

Today's desktop computers have millions of parts called **transistors** that decode, or process, hundreds of instructions from a computer program. Consoles have a special RISC (Reduced Instruction Set Computing) computer chip. This needs more instructions than those in an ordinary desktop computer, but it is simpler. This means the computer can carry out instructions far more quickly.

What's Next?

Some video games use virtual reality to make the players feel as if they are part of the images they see. The players wear headsets that show slightly different images to each eye. This creates the illusion of a three-dimensional scene in which the player can move around.

Video games that use virtual reality make players feel as though they are in a three-dimensional action scene.

BIG POOLS, LITTLE POOLS

Some swimmers take pride in breaking the ice in order to enjoy their midwinter swim. But you're probably not one of them! Most people prefer to swim in warmer waters in the sunshine or in an indoor pool where the weather doesn't matter. Large water parks with artificial warm climates are becoming very popular in places where it is hard to predict the weather. The water in all these pools has to be kept warm. But bacteria (disease-carrying germs) multiply easily in warm, wet conditions, so the water also has to be cleaned regularly.

Keeping the Heat In

Like the hot water in your house, the water in many pools is heated using gas or electricity. But this is very expensive. Some pools are now heated using solar panels. Solar panels are sheets of metal that are painted black and enclosed in glass sheets. This helps them to absorb heat from the sun. The pool water is pumped through tubes in the panels to heat it up. At night, when there is no heat from the sun, the water begins to cool. One way to prevent this is to cover the water with hollow plastic balls at night. The air inside the balls is an excellent **insulator.** It acts as a barrier, trapping heat in the water for longer periods.

You can have lots of fun at the world's biggest swimming pool on the Japanese island of Kyushu.

Sparkling Clean

In the fall, outdoor pools have to be cleared of leaves. And the water from any pool has to be cleaned and filtered all year around to remove dirt and other garbage. The water is pumped out of the pool through a filter unit that acts like a sieve. It is then pumped back into the pool. However, a water filter does not remove bacteria or tiny plants called algae. These plants, if left alone, can grow so much that they turn the water green. Both the bacteria and algae are killed by a chemical called chlorine, which is a strong bleach. It is added in tiny amounts to the water.

Under the Water

An aquarium is a pool for fish and underwater creatures. It is made out of glass or see-through plastic so that you can look inside. To get a really good look at the fish, you need to get up-close with them. To make this possible, some modern aquariums have a walkway inside a long plastic tube that runs along the bottom of the tank. The circular shape of the tube makes it very strong. It is able to handle the pressure of the water pushing on it.

At Osaka Aquarium in Japan, these children get really close to all kinds of underwater creatures.

TELEVISION WORLD

When was the last time you watched television? Yesterday afternoon? Last night? This morning? We can come home at any time, switch on the television, sit back, and watch any number of shows. It is hardly surprising then that television is the most popular form of entertainment, watched by many millions of people all over the world! Color television is the result of 50 years of research. The first televisions showed a black-and-white picture made up of only a few lines on a small circular screen. Today's color televisions have screens of all sizes, produce high-quality sound, and show pictures with lifelike color, enabling people to have a theater in their own homes.

Nowadays even people who attend an event can see the main action from wherever they sit or stand televised on enormous screens.

TELEVISION VIEWING

In 1926 a Scottish engineer, John Logie Baird (1886–1946), gave the first demonstration of a television system. He became famous overnight. But it took another 10 years before the first regular television programs were made.

Inside a Television

The back of a television screen is coated with millions of tiny dots, arranged in lines in groups of three. These dots are made of chemical substances called phosphors, which glow when struck by a beam of electrons (particles charged with negative electricity). A color television has three beams that come from electron guns at the back of the television. When hit by the beams, one phosphor dot in each group glows red, one glows blue, and the other green. When you look at the screen from a distance, your eyes combine the red, blue, and green light to form a clear color picture.

Television in Orbit

Most television programs are sent as signals from TV stations or transmitters and are picked up by television aerials. These signals travel in straight lines. They cannot "bend" over mountains or around the earth. For this reason, different cities have their own local television stations or transmitters. However, communications **satellites** in space can transmit television signals all around the world. Geostationary satellites (satellites with orbits that keep them exactly over the same place on earth) beam television programs directly to satellite dishes. They can transmit television programs between different countries around the world or send many programs to one country.

There are three electron guns at the back of a television set. They are directed onto the phosphor dots very precisely by **electromagnets.**

MIXING LIGHT

Most colors can be produced by mixing red, blue, and green light in different amounts. Equal amounts of red and green light make yellow; red and blue make magenta; blue and green make cyan; all three colors together make white. All the images you see on a color television or film are made by mixing different amounts of red, blue, and green light.

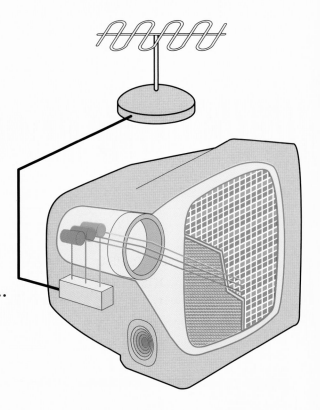

DIVE! DIVE! DIVE!

Would you like the chance to explore an underwater city or an ancient shipwreck? The ocean bed hides all sorts of fascinating secrets. In the last 50 years, the sport of diving has gradually begun to open this underwater world to thousands of people. The latest advances in equipment have made diving safer and more popular than ever before. But divers have always faced two related problems—finding a way to breathe under water and dealing with the crushing pressure of the water at great depths. What are the solutions to these problems?

Breathing Under Water

The deeper divers go under the ocean, the greater the weight, or pressure, of the water on their chests, and the harder it is to breathe. This problem has been solved for people diving down to about 100 feet by the invention of SCUBA (Self-Contained Underwater Breathing Apparatus). The diver breathes air that has been forced, or compressed, into a steel tank at about 300 times **atmospheric pressure.** Before this air passes into the diver's mouthpiece, it goes through a **valve,** which reduces the pressure until it exactly matches the pressure of the surrounding water. This enables the diver to breathe easily.

SCUBA

A French naval officer, Jacques Ives Cousteau (b.1910), perfected the aqualung diving apparatus (1943), now called SCUBA. It enabled him, and countless others who followed him, to explore under water free from the heavy traditional diving suit.

SCUBA divers explore coral reefs, underwater caves, and glaciers. They also enjoy seeing underwater life up close.

Decompression

One of the gases we breathe is called nitrogen. When divers are deep under water, high pressure causes the nitrogen in their air supply to dissolve in their blood. When they return to the surface the nitrogen is released. If they come back up suddenly, the nitrogen is released too quickly, and the divers suffer a paralyzing condition called the bends. Returning to the surface slowly allows nitrogen to leave harmlessly. This process is called decompression.

BARREL SUIT

In 1721 John Lethbridge invented a diving suit shaped like a barrel. It had two holes for arms and a glass peephole, so the diver could see under water. The diver lay facedown, and had to return to the surface to breathe.

UNDER PRESSURE

Although we cannot feel it, the weight of the air above us presses down on our bodies. This pressure is measured in atmospheres. On dry land, the air we breathe normally has a pressure of 1 atmosphere. Water pressure is also measured in atmospheres. The further down you go under the water, the greater the pressure. In the ocean, water pressure increases by 1 atmosphere every 33 feet.

In 1960 the *Bathyscaphe* descended 8 miles into the deepest part of the Pacific Ocean, where the water pressure is more than 1,000 atmospheres. The *Bathyscaphe's* shape made it strong enough to withstand water pressure that would crush any ordinary vessel.

SAIL POWER

When you think of sailing, do you picture a small boat or yacht cutting across the waves, sails stretched in the breeze? Sailing can be a very relaxing pastime—but not always. Ice yachts, which "sail" on ice, are the fastest of all sail-powered crafts, sometimes achieving speeds of more than 140 mph. The fastest sailing vessels on water regularly reach about 50 mph, often in winds of no more than about 20 mph. How is this possible?

Modern sailing vessels, like this catamaran and sailboard, are built from tough, light materials. Their designs cleverly use the driving force of the wind and the resistance of the water in which they float to get the maximum possible forward speed.

TRIANGLE OF FORCES

A sailing yacht "reaches" or sails across the wind. The wind pushing on the sails produces a force that acts in two directions. It pushes the yacht forward and tries to push it sideways at the same time. The yacht's center board, or keel, resists the sideways push and converts it into a forward pushing force. The three forces—the wind, the sideways force, and the resulting forward force—acting together are called the **triangle of forces**.

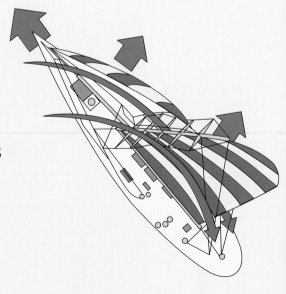

Modern sailing vessels are built from tough, lightweight materials for greater strength and speed. The hulls, or frame, of sailboats such as the International Laser are built out of GRP (glass-reinforced plastic). GRP consists of layers of matting made from fine strands of glass. The layers of matting are cut to shape and placed in a mold. Then they are soaked in a synthetic resin—a liquid, plastic material that sets very hard. Together, the resin and glass fibers make a very strong material. The different parts of the hull are made in separate molds and are then glued together. This makes the hull watertight. As long as the hull remains undamaged, these boats are almost unsinkable.

More than 100,000 International Lasers have been built. These fast racing sailboats are constructed from glass fiber and are almost unsinkable. Their **spars** are made of aluminum **alloys** or carbon fiber, and their sails from Mylar—a strong synthetic plastic material.

LAND YACHTS

In Mauritania in Western Africa, sail-powered craft race along on railroad tracks at high speeds. These specialized land yachts achieve speeds of more than 100 mph, but they are easily blown over, because they run on rails. They cannot be steered out of danger of falling over like a sailboat can.

WAVE ACTION

What does the phrase "a day at the beach" mean to you? For some people, it means a day in the sun, fishing, swimming, playing beach games, and relaxing. For others it means a day pitting their skills against the waves. If the waves are big enough, surfers balancing on surfboards can ride them at astonishing speed, keeping just ahead of the crests of the waves. Further out to sea, sailboarders can test their strength against the energy of the wind and waves. What causes waves? And how can surfers go so fast?

Wind and Waves

If you look at waves coming in toward a beach, you will notice that in deeper water the waves travel toward the shore, usually without breaking. But as they ride up toward the shore, they tumble over and crash onto the beach. This is because the bottom of the wave is dragged along the sand and slowed down. But the top of the wave continues at speed, so it topples over in the shallower water on the beach.

TSUNAMIS

Violent storms or underwater earthquakes can cause freak waves that are more than 95 feet high. These waves are often called tidal waves. Scientists prefer the Japanese name, *tsunamis,* because such waves are not caused by tides. Tsunamis begin far out at sea and can become very dangerous. As they approach land they speed up and may cause great destruction on shore.

These surfers in Hawaii manage to keep just ahead of the waves that push them at incredible speeds.

Small and Fast

Surfboards and sailboards plane. This means they skim over the surface of the water. They can go as fast as the person riding them dares to! In fact, some boards are so small and light they will not float when the rider is still, because they are not **buoyant** enough. They sink under the rider's weight. They can only support their rider when traveling on the crest of a wave at great speed, because they can plane on top of the surface.

Modern sand yachts that can top 78 mph first appeared in Belgium in the 1920s. However, in the 300s BC, the Emperor Liang Yuan Ti of China had a wind cart made that could carry 30 passengers.

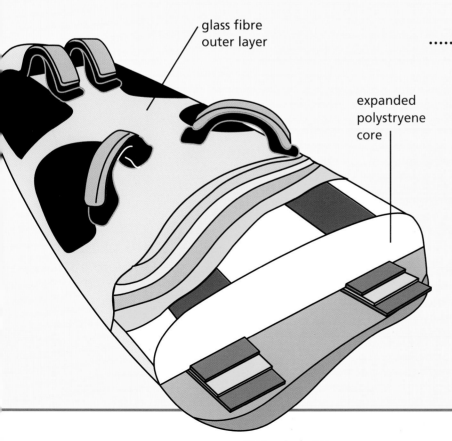

glass fibre outer layer

expanded polystryene core

A surfboard must be strong and lightweight. The core, or inside, is made of expanded polystyrene, a foamlike plastic that can be carved into any shape. Glass fiber and carbon fiber on the outside make the boards strong enough to withstand the beating of waves.

FREE AS A BIRD

Have you ever dreamed that you could fly? Flying a hang glider must be the nearest thing to it! Experienced hang glider pilots have been launched from hot-air balloons, have been towed into the air, or have jumped over cliffs. When they are airborne, hang glider pilots seek out rising currents of warmer air called thermals. Once caught in a thermal, the hangglider may rise many thousands of feet into the air and is capable of flying great distances.

Hang gliders have an aluminum frame, shaped like the letter A, that is both strong and light. Depending on the type of glider, the wing is formed by stretching flexible or rigid material over the A-frame. The pilot hangs from a harness below the wing, safely attached to it by a karabiner—a strong metal clip. This special clip was originally invented for mountaineers, who use it to attach themselves to ropes. Because it is closed by a spring, it can be quickly opened.

THERMALS

Thermals often happen in warm, thundery weather. Air is heated by the sun and rises, because it is lighter than the surrounding cold air. The cold air pushes under the warm air, causing it to rise. Thermals help gliders fly long distances by lifting them up high in the sky. Gliders cannot climb by themselves and drop quickly if they are not being lifted by a thermal.

The pilot steers the hang glider by holding onto an A-frame and making side-to-side body movements.

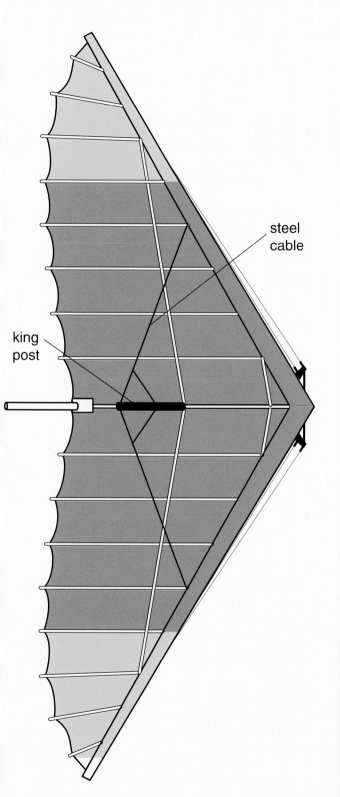

king
post

steel
cable

A hang glider is made even stronger by steel cables stretched under tension (very tightly) to the wing and a post at the center called the king post. The cables prevent the wing from bending too much and breaking. Weights are placed on the wing to test it for strength. These weights are equal to six times any force that the hang glider is likely to encounter.

EARLY GLIDERS

Otto Lilienthal (1849–1896), a German, made hundreds of short flights in homemade gliders that he designed and built out of willow and cotton. He launched himself from hilltops and controlled his direction by body movements, like modern hang glider pilots do. Lilienthal studied bird-flight closely, and his machines were very similar to the first designs for a flying machine sketched by the great artist and sculptor Leonardo da Vinci in about 1487. Before his death in a flying accident, Lilienthal made a flight of more than 1,100 feet.

GLOSSARY

acoustics the science of sound

alloy a mixture of two or more metals

aluminum a very light, strong metal

atmospheric pressure the weight of the air around us

binary digits a system of numbers using only 0 and 1 to represent all the numbers instead of units, 10's, and 100's, and so on. For example, 1 is 001, 2 is 0010, 4 is 0100.

buoyant capable of floating

cable strong wires by which force is used to control or operate a mechanism

calorie unit used to measure heat energy units used by scientists to measure work or energy

cantilever supporting link between brake cables and brake pads

carbon fiber a very pure and fine fiber made of carbon. It is used to reinforce plastic materials to make them strong.

centripetal force the force you feel when you whirl a weight on string around and around

electromagnet core of magnetic material surrounded by a coil of wire, through which an electric current is passed to magnetize the core

fiberglass strong plastic material reinforced with matting made from finely spun glass fibers, sometimes called GRP or glass reinforced plastic

friction the rubbing of one thing against another and the force that resists it

game console a combination of a display and keyboard or switches by which a player can interact with a computer game

graphics pictures produced by a computer

gravity a force or pull between any two objects such as the earth and an apple falling toward it

hydraulic a mechanism, such as a brake, operated by a liquid in a pipe

insulator a material that keeps you warm because it does not conduct heat

nylon a tough, lightweight plastic material used to make fabrics

perspiration sweat

satellite a kind of automatic television station sent into space by rocket to travel around the world to send television pictures back to earth. It is also used for telephone transmission.

spar in this case, the mast used to support the sail

synthetic produced artificially rather than occurring naturally

titanium a metal added to steel to make it strong and able to withstand high temperatures

transistor an electronic device that is used to amplify (make stronger) an electric current or to switch it on and off

triangle of forces a method used by physicists to add to the effect of two forces acting in different directions

valve a device like a faucet used to turn something, such as air or water, on and off and control its flow

virtual reality pictures controlled or generated by a computer, which appear to be real and in which the viewer seems to be involved

FACT FILE

- The first computer game to go on sale was developed in 1971 by Nolan Bushnell, a young engineer. It was called *Computer Space* and barely sold 2,000 copies. Bushnell's next game, *Pong,* a form of table tennis, was a huge success and sold more than 100,000 copies. Bushnell went on to open Atari, the computer company.

- Hang gliding started when Francis Melvin Rogallo designed a strong, flexible wing in 1948. But it was an Australian engineer, Bill Moyes, who produced the familiar delta-shaped wing. In 1969 Moyes's partner, Bill Bennet, tested the design. He was towed on water skis and took off to fly over the Statue of Liberty.

- Captain Cooke, the explorer and navigator, described surfing in Hawaii in 1771. Surfing became popular in California during the 1950s and 1960s.

- The longest sailing vessel ever built is the French *Club Med 1.* This ship has five aluminum masts, and the 2,500 square feet of sails are computer-controlled. However, the *Cheng Ho,* a massive Chinese vessel built in about 1420, is believed to have had nine masts.

- The earliest bicycle race (for which records exist) took place at the Parc de St. Cloud in Paris, France in 1868.

- Sega, Sony, and five other large entertainment companies are involved in location-based entertainment centers, or LBEs. These provide theaters, theme park rides, and video games in one place. Cinetropolis centers are an example of an LBE. Here, film rides are shown on wrap-around screens. The seats are coordinated to move with the film, about three feet in any direction—enough to give anyone the illusion of terrifying movement!

FURTHER READINGS

Cobb, Vicki. *Sneakers Meet Your Feet.* Little, Brown, 1985.

Gibbons, Gail. *Bicycle Book.* Holiday, 1995.

Holden, Paul. *Wind and Surf.* Lerner Publication Company, 1991.

INDEX